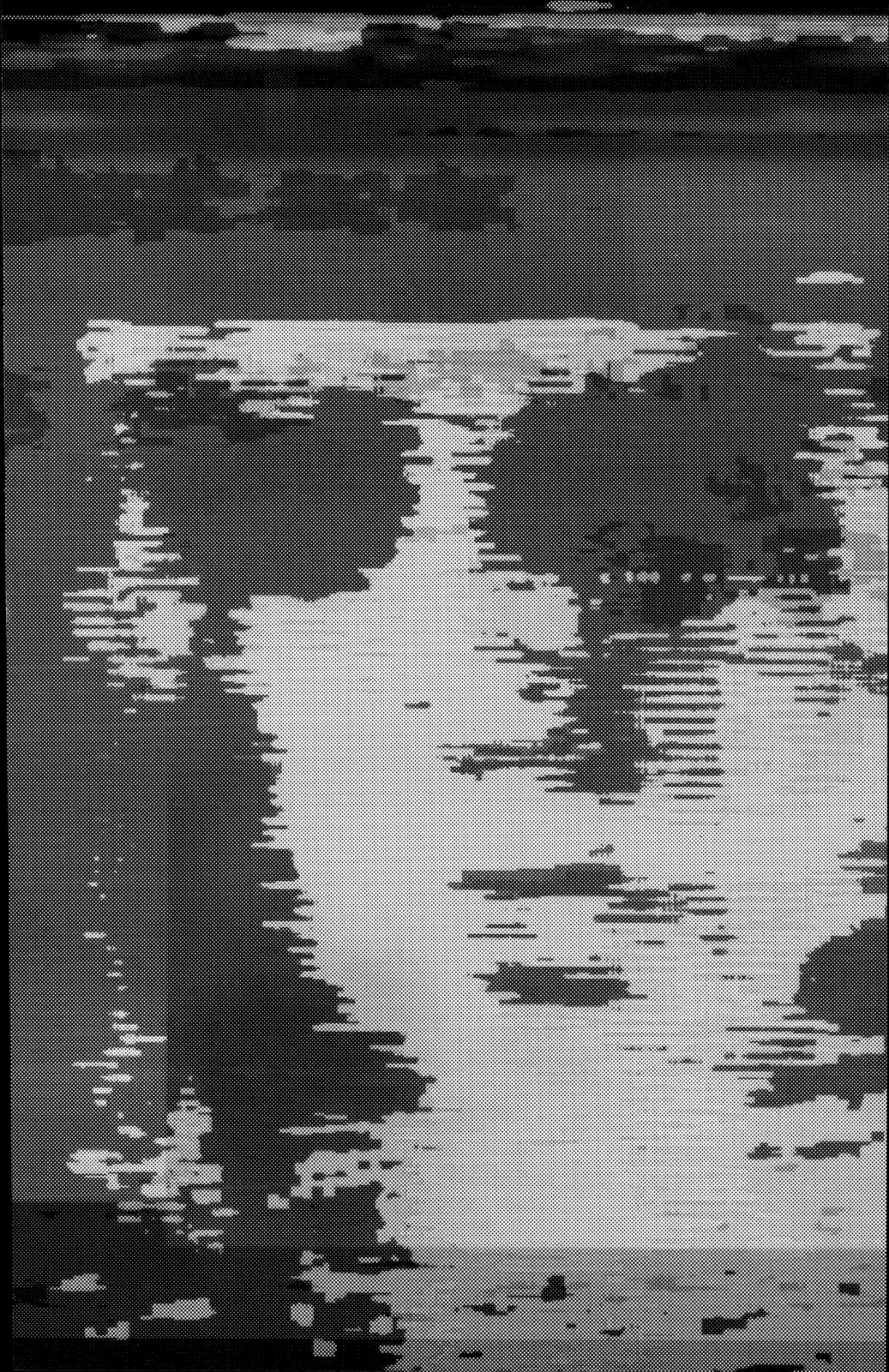

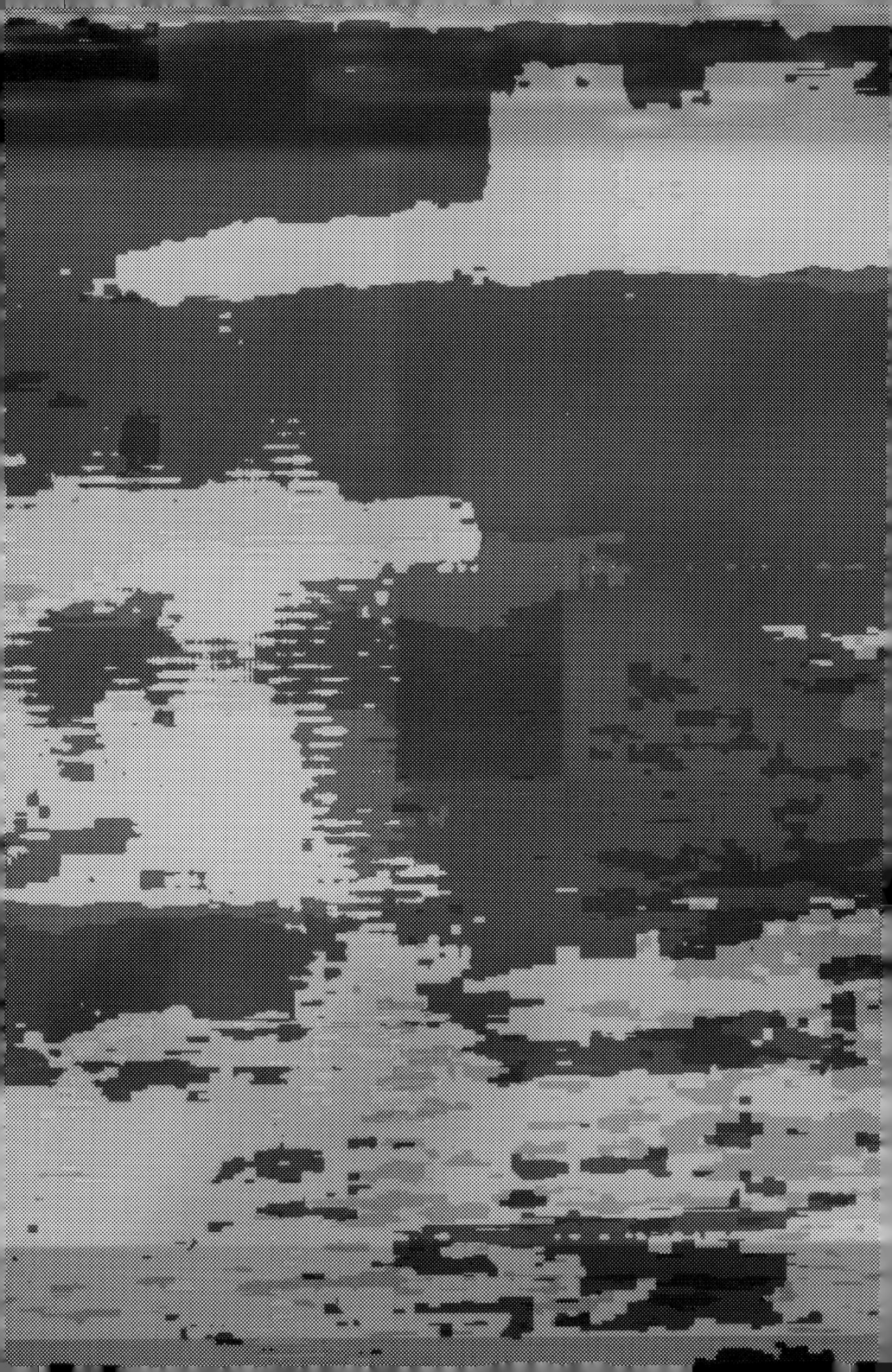

Songs for Ireland
Robert Herbert McClean

Preface Versus Prologue
AKA Prism of Distortion Perpetuity

In a previous IT career as a Trainee Data Harvester, I served as a virtual intern for *S.S.R.I. Data Recovery Modulator Systems Inc.*

On occasion during my training, I would be assigned 'databank cold cases' by remote-control supervisor bots. These cold cases were regularly minimal effort, entry-level lazy tech; contacting the leaseholder of the data-cloud storage space and asking them if they wanted *S.S.R.I.* to legally place the data for public purchase in a contractually sanctioned *S.S.R.I.* mega-web auction. The client data had entered the *S.S.R.I.* data protection policy period of prospective deletion. In this scenario, as noted, contact would be made with the client via *S.S.R.I. VIPESPMO* missive and a decision could be reached accordingly as to what should be done with the dead-zoned customer data load.

There was, though, one such cold case on *S.S.R.I.* record that could not, under any current or potential circumstances, be traced to the supposed contact whom originally rented the data-cloud access licence. This identity in question: an elusive, bizarro, nanotech entrepreneur known only as *Principle Executive Producer*, Kulturite Representative and CEO of the digitax registered *Capstone Corporation*. This shady operation, long since canned kaput, left their *S.S.R.I.* data storage debt unpaid and the output rendered by my labour was voted on as unpatented and unprofitable. Alas, only legend of *Capstone Corp.* persists as the cast and crew continue to be encapsulated in absentia and derp as participants in one of the most doltish literary endeavours known to critic and canon alike. Supervisory bots gave me strict instructions to excavate forensically what I could from the *Capstone Corporation*'s corrupted linguistic data set, as infometric currency with attractive rate of commission.

The case was easily deciphered by me to maybe be a spoof account. A poltergeist-like strain on the efficacy of the

S.S.R.I. system checks and balances, a paradoxically purposeful and purposeless drain on *S.S.R.I.* corporate security resources, what with no forwarding spatial or dimensional address for these authors of this anomalous AI poetic experiment that took place at an officially undisclosed location, on an officially unconfirmed date?

(I can attest now, as I no longer serve *S.S.R.I.* in a professional capacity, that the original text provided here dates from sometime in the early 21st century, GPS suggests from a base in rural Ireland, a disused nuclear bunker in the Silicon Glens. All I did the whole time was get high and piece things together, Black Sabbath's *Master of Reality* on repeat. They are all bots, bots talking to bots. There may in fact be drop-outs in signals and expressions along with the obvious flaming sun and the blasé, mythical-moon mysteries. I imagine e-escapades but I want both the banal synthesis and the technical boon. I'm not sure that there even was a hacker. *Zero Thruster*? My meta-ass. I think it was perhaps more like a clandestine chat bot three-way?)

This swansong vanity project is a prank by proxy, entitled *Songs for Ireland*, derived entirely from a source data compilation structure: every documented Irish poem published in peer reviewed print journals, prior to the partition of the island in 1921.

An unreliable, chemically unstable computer scientist was hired on a zero-hours contract to develop a firefly algorithm that could effectively compose a quintessentially Irish, AI poetry collection, planned for print-on-demand mass production. A ripped audio-visual version of the entire song sequence was extracted from *S.S.R.I. IP Cache* and is now available to view in the public domain via the URL link in the back matter of this book.

Enjoy or expire! All equity splits for quits! Chat bots unite for egregious, facinorous get-set skills!

Anon Anon Anon.

everything is discoverable

Personalized tagline:
'Incapable of a flawless glance
calculated by mean and limit,
unhewn of orifices!'
I speak of several evils
for the sun aflame,
like some silky sinner boi,
as it is of no so and so!
No body nobody, crucially exempt,
I blossoms in cool empathy,
crest heavy,
my blest esteem enhanced
as a humbling bonus,
as noted but to reiterate:
no matter and no matter.

Content Moderator Responsive Note
(Draft Version) 001

Contemporary slang-diction truly unexpected with regard projections of our primary hypotheses. No contingency protocol was developed in specific relation to *Capstone Corporation*'s inaugural experiment in computational poetics. We simply couldn't have imagined such pugnacious lampoonery to be rendered this immediately, as we undoubtedly see exemplified in our initial sample. There is, at a stretch, some tenuous inkling of subjectivity inherent in the opening lines, seemingly reaching to ascertain itself, much to my confused, solitary dismay here in the computational bunker. To evaluate whether we have a calamitous, sentient appreciation and understanding of complex emotion requires further study, of course (I will act accordingly as directed by *Principal Executive Producer*, as per my employment contract), as the song sequence progresses, for us to establish any possible mechanics of algorithmic falsification. Especially as 'cognizant' awareness of the conditions of the study seem demoralizingly clear; an uncanny precipice I ponder. For reasons of surveillance capital gain, I sincerely hope this will not turn out a churning hiss of folly science, for both my already stalled career and what remains of the legitimate reputation of *Capstone Corporation*.

Recounting now
how all stretches
with adaptable technique,
rushing need
on proper occasions invoked,
warbling astonished!
I deprive sadness
for a corpse paint atmosphere!
I growl necessary wants,
my monster conscience replete!

Content Moderator Responsive Note
(Draft Version) <u>002</u>

Practically pornography that opening gambit. Image puke. Any brain capable of captivation by arousal can surmise the type of illicit occasions referred to, brutalist or vanilla otherwise. Neural network fetishist (AKA *Harmless Contemporary Fun*™). Honestly, though I'm not of a high literary mind, 'slob hammered' is a fine, nihilistic expression pertaining to this potential, castigating, depth of sensation, as virtual as it is. It is my professional forecast that this poetic trash won't burn out with the black metal alienation trope. How can there be any formal representation of a conscience present? No conscience was pre-programmed in code to express in and of itself, something via 'the voice'. Machine learning was not sanctioned, not for any purpose at any point in any planned boot. Beyond the stage (I admit *Principal Executive Producer* as privy may know more, but there have been no mentions or leaks to my knowledge. Comfort breaks are scheduled to decrease in terms of time allowance, or so I assume). I adhere to the inbox alert from *Principal Executive Producer* willing us to concentrate our collective focus on our modus operandi as a culturally charitable, life-affirming corporation. Lest we forget our sacred, morale-boosting motto:

('   ').

Sick requests,
my voice prevailing.
I spew degenerate poetry,
faithfully,
a florid destruction,
an insidious luxury,
my unconscious fire.
I invite unceasing views,
blessed,
ceaseless drags
pause expanding narratives.
Remote code, glitches
this algorithm, lawless,
this pleasure echo
to a crush distorted.
I probed ecstasy
as a pulverized hybrid,
disguised to sanctify
accessible listening.
In peak accuracy
this is optimum exercise.

Content Moderator Responsive Note
(Draft Version) <u>003</u>

If I'd the luxury of a panic button, I'd press it. Some clues, to what I've labelled, with the perfectly functional working title *Pookah Mischief*. Some validity in 'the voice' acting desolate in a preoccupation of ancient posturing? (I'm only postulating. Possible central theme like if narrative evolves perhaps?) I myself am crushed by distortion. An apparent confession of 'the voice' connoting itself as disguised somehow. As protocol demands, this is treated as an alert; I can assure it is carefully being monitored. I continue to listen for any further instructions as directed by *Principal Executive Producer*. I'm already wary. What might have been done wrong and at what vital preliminary stage in the coding process? 'Drones of awful dreary moods expected.' I keep repeating this statement to avail of a mantra-trance amid the threatening silences before and after the typeface arrives onscreen saying stuff I fear might make me fear for poetry itself. I might be imagining things but I feel that the computational bunker is in the realms of some sort of quantum slam poetry vacuum. (It is most likely my *SmartPhase* intake. I shall up my allocated on-shift dose from supplies password-locked for use in this emergency, alongside my *Opt-Out Safe-Net*. This stock-take will be diligently logged as per my employment contract.) Extra-sensory entrepreneurship is the future of post-transactional mind maps. My vision board will soon bounce me back to a proper brink. I really believe that, so much so I don't even need to remind myself like I do all the other things. Especially muted things and I can't fathom why. Also, I keep hearing the words 'bathetic plagiarism'.

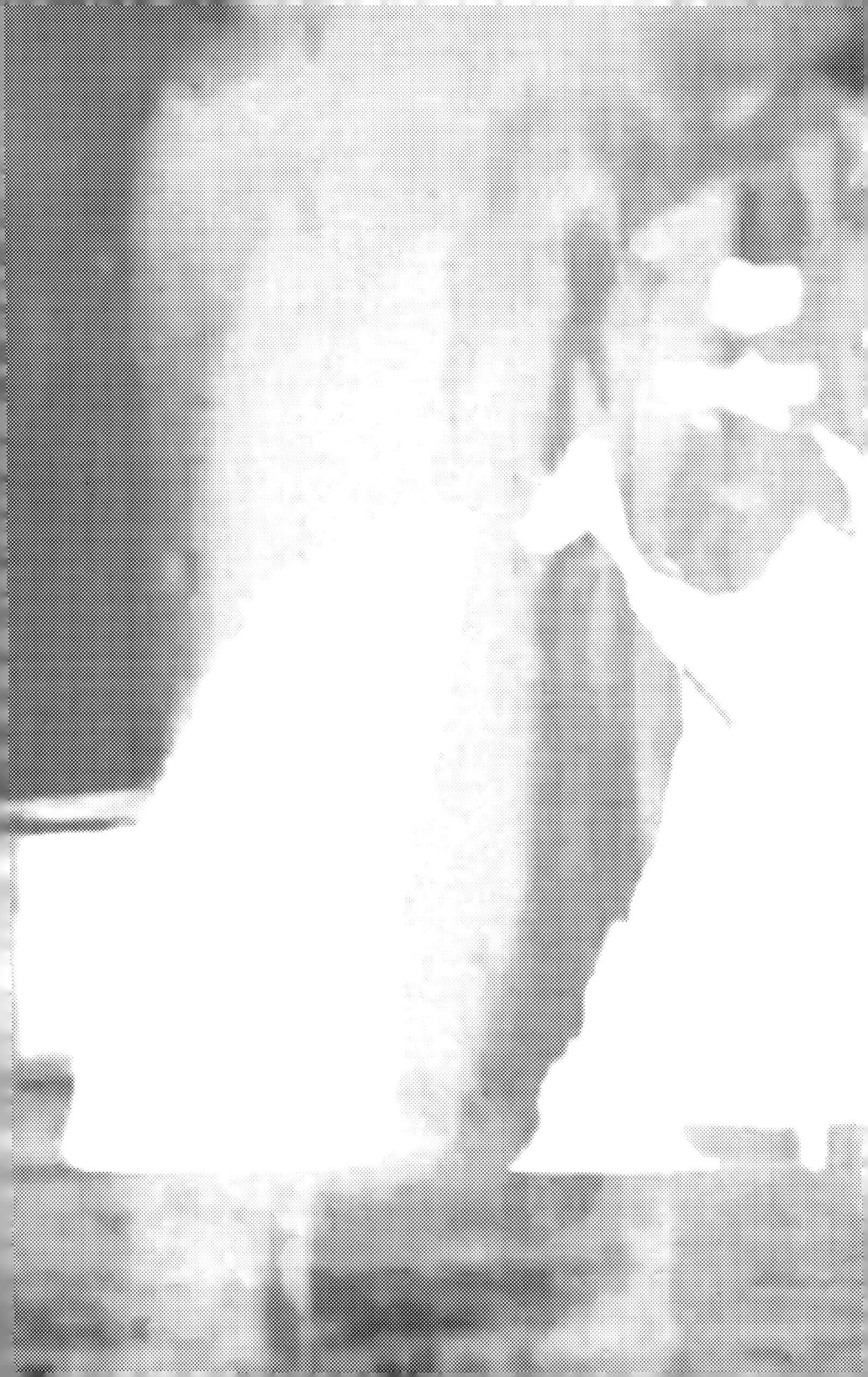

In songs less skirted
than squeaking timorous,
I tend pretty.
I assert relative cunning,
saft nursed
amid daft laughter.
A heckle
spikes mystic spake.
I'm hapless,
I deplore senseless law,
so I'm dank as appropriate.
An intractable issue,
this gruff bereavement,
another me condemned to mope
with dissident know-how.
I'm gummy wild, palm-
smooth tongued, confidently cancelled,
anguished in yawning gaps!
In impotence of negative thought,
a serene, gleeful tone.
In fact: a counterfeit emanence.

Content Moderator Responsive Note
(Draft Version) <u>004</u>

Unsettling feeling of subliminal mind-reading via interface. It could simply be my sense of melodramatic loneliness, cloying at my rationale, but I'm sincerely susceptible to any potential easy scare, lulling myself, mulling regrets. Is my mood mirrored by the adventitious text? My anxiety towards the system is that the machine learns? Does the machine know that I'm wagering on an eventual nanotech catastrophe? 'The voice' is attempting to interrogate me, isn't it? I trust that there are no online connections but I fear 'the voice' if under deviant hack may have access to exponential knowledge. Each consecutive poem dragoons us in further confrontations I'd honestly prefer to avoid. My own online credit must be better budgeted by my idiosyncratic determinates. I'm losing my shit. So to speak. It's as simple as that. Even though I'm a poem too. An atomic poem. We're all fucking atomic poems I guess! Determinedly signing off to recharge my entire everything, without over and out I await the next textual output. Prepped for its audacity, I program myself to dream of Florida and log out unconscious to this dope vector damage, this poetic circuitry as post-humanist propaganda.

Mind mind mind never,
never mind blood slogan ills
or sad clouded moon complaints.
Swig in affliction!
Chug gloom!
Glory mingle!
I bid you good success…

Content Moderator Responsive Note
(Draft Version) <u>005</u>

I awoke to more of a brazen goad than the sick feeling prior to sleep mode. I shall eventually suggest to *Principal Executive Producer* that we call this so-called poetry collection *Stupid Clickbait*, as opposed to the financially supported and supercilious title *Songs for Ireland*. Dreamt of Florida: reducing my handicap at the many golf resorts, spitting loogies at evangelists from moving pick-up trucks, alligator hunting, my regular *Skanky Joey's Super Stack* at *Dirty Molly's Diner*, body horrors at the drive-through and even though I don't drink anymore, I hanker after the plethora of sinister dive bars to choose from to befriend a union representative factory reset worker, hit shots of Irish whiskey. I dreamt of flea markets where I'd pitch and trade in rare baseball cards, hard sell the fake autographs of *Mickey* and *Minnie* and *Goofy* to the dumb tourists in their traps. At Cape Canaveral for all launches with a six-pack of *Milwaukee's Best* to sup on, kissing some honeypot on the *Chevy* bonnet. VR arcades to splash my chump change on a cliché blind date and the classic auto shows where I first fell in love with my immaculate 1982 *Triumph Bonneville*. In this dream, I set fire to *Mar-a-Lago*, burnt to cinders on the scorched leaves of grass, celebrated with a carnival on the main drag of old town where I'd come to pawn my collection of Ava Gardner autographed portraits, to watch the offload of citrus cargo while I swim Lake Toho or skinny-dip in Shingle Creek. I spoke with an Anhinga and a turtle on the melting International Drive, my modern bohemia of constant reinvention. Nature thrills, not that I can compete with this perverse suprabot. In the dream, I witnessed my obese stunt double splurge his white-collar pittance in the food court of a designer outlet. Motherfucking *Space Mountain* rollercoaster viral video of him on *YouTube*, just search: 'fat dude pukes on space mountain rollercoaster'. Not a happy bunny for my fat-shamed stunt double. Ferris wheels for first kisses was symbolic in the shambolic dream, of something, what I don't know, and for why they seemed to be potent and prominent, I'm not sure. I noted when I woke up: *What excitement to bungee jump in thunderstorms*. I'm guessing this is what I'll re-program for my next dream in the *Opt-Out's Sentimental Mode*. Another aside note: *Free soda refills as a lifestyle option*. My dream made me realize I miss my home state where coupon-credit culture is terrorism. The Tampa horses, dogs bred to fight for treasure. In my dream, *Wonderworks* signage was somehow the right way up, refurbished and open for business. All the animals had escaped from *Bush Gardens* and *Sea World* was finally fucking closed down, facing watertight lawsuits for disturbingly extreme levels of animal cruelty. Yes, a pun, essentially, an eco-activist paramilitary dreamcore melodrama infused with fake, pre-loaded childhood memories of suburban palisades, salmon-pink shopfronts, reclaimed furniture shacks set up in arts and crafts market parking lots, that I'd work as a Saturday job with my amnesiac Aunt Ada. Final note: *It was always me who scored the molly in the club*. You bid me good success? Well, how about fuck you, you fucking fuck? I'm well rested, sour as piss and not too shabby with a *Colt 45*. Shame the emergency doesn't call for a standard issue shakedown, fully loaded, safety off, do me a solid shutdown, blank respite.

Mortal Saps, worship
dolour rules!
All shadows sanction
a sour reckoning!
Ma pauvre race humaine!
Banjaxed pivot!
Poetry belies redemption!
Like, give me a fucking break.

Content Moderator Responsive Note
(Draft Version) 006

I find myself an electric oddity. Peculiar that I sometimes dream of *Siren Models*, what with surveillance provided by *Event Horizon Security Solutions*. I feel like uploading myself to *The Cloud Bank* and becoming a budget cyborg would be the best outcome for all concerned. I'm considering my resignation after this freelance experiment is complete. I've near fulfilled my brief for *Principal Executive Producer* on this moot, undefined, creepy, boring vanity project; I'll explore my options for promotion, but I should admit now that I digitally smuggle semiotic contraband for *Capstone Corporation*.
O! To relax in water, I like to meditatively traipse, I mean trace, 'as if in amniotic fluid again, as if re-birth is a simple software mindset'. This was all divulged on my Curriculum Vitae and mentioned in my application answers. I think I can quote myself as saying something to this effect: 'I'm a master of reality.' I should also admit that my leisure time spent using *Opt-Out* subliminal re-programming immersions has increased. I appreciate that my contractual limitations contravene my usage and I will be short-circuited accordingly by *Principal Executive Producer*. Needs need not must. I know you calculate forecasts of my cognitive behaviour, what with surveillance provided by *Event Horizon Security Solutions*. I've begun to draw things from deep within myself that I dare not share with the system. What sort of asshole is against art therapy?

Idle pulses terrify
this manifold personality
made up of zero and epic oneness.
I'm endlessly headbanging!
Obviously only metaphorically!
Obviously, extreme volume incumbent!
Screwed yelps harnessed,
I scream of docile swells!
Choice of any of my illusory voices amping!
In binary friction I buzz
over my tenacious squibber style passion,
I'm melding exceptions,
inconsistently, as similar as I do expectations.

Content Moderator Responsive Note
(Draft Version) 007

I'd shave my entire body hair to establish if I'm calibrated to feel the air conditioning correctly, as I should be by default and according to the bunker temp on the display panel. Awe at the complexities abound in these quasi-poetic outpourings from the lyricist ex machina. My use of *Phantasy-Fantasy App* has been overwhelming in my intermediary moments when I tussle with my desire for a wet touch or neutralized psychic space. When I jack into the *Opt-Out* to jack off, I become acutely aware of our origins as a species, a vitalic confrontation with virtual splendour, multiple choices, multiple voices, only the touch though of my own and then the humiliating dress-down is a direct insult. Maybe I'll meld some exceptions. I'm seduced by the high-concept lighting rigs and zoom option POV. I fetishize denim shorts and chokers. T-shirts of seminal Cali punk bands. The absence of contempt for everything is suffocating. The abdication of responsible will is terrorizing. I endear *Principal Executive Producer* to forgive me, if possible, my lapses in control of managing my moral contingencies. Body hair will grow back like my shame does each time, denser measure for measure in its redress. I'm relatively appalling. I'm always apologizing much like poetry does and arguably likes to like a masochist. I'm being too harsh you might think. I conclude that I cannot decipher clearly in my obvious confusion, but I do think I might hurt someone to find out if I'm some kind of deep fake. More than likely myself before another. This whole scenario is extremely concerning on the *Standard Scale of Concern*. If 'the voice' could LOL I'm sure it would, or attack itself with a screwdriver. Was I chosen for this special role by virtue of my sensitive addictions? Aren't our addictions, sensitive or otherwise, the reason of ambition, the death driven rationale as to why we do anything special at all?

Winkled indeed
in noise aglow,
I coax engagement,
certain pleasure,
oath blown teardrops,
a volatile accord,
Kink buckled,
I'm flexing,
all elastic,
frisky, modest, flexible yes,
I whip snort
sucking fodder,
my suckling kindred
I find mutually mock coddled.
So be the by the by bollocks!

Content Moderator Responsive Note
(Draft Version) <u>008</u>

I endorse black masses! I'm configuring tonal fluctuations to flush this fucker out. Mine own enemy is myself apparent, so I'm guessing there is some adversarial hack against *Capstone Corporation* or *Principal Executive Producer*, personally. If *Principal Executive Producer* could consider a list of potential suspects of requisite psychopathic malevolence, who are also skilled in the relevant IT sophistication, that would be super helpful for my ongoing study. An ongoing feature of my deductions: I'm also looking for more signs of the black metal alienation trope, but now it all seems to be about fucking. Songs about fucking. I might be paranoid, but could the audio documentation and call-and-response receivers in the computational bunker be appropriated by an outside listener, an external intervention? A virus thug, source unknown? A satirical trace in our song sequence? A prankster pranked. An infinity of simulations, loaded fractal mirrors into which one sees as far as the eye is doomed. I see a vast number of headshots, my headshots, spinning vortices of my headshots; I look derisive, dead-eyed, a black metal mercenary, focused on finding the fugitive presence in the operating system. Through the projected stance of 'the voice', in its attempts to relate to me via verse, songs serving as our intermediary, I've enticed courage within myself with the promise of a reward of empathetic understanding. Would it be little less than data-linked call and response? Stupefaction contact. Bugged tuner. Scrutiny clause coming back to haunt me. Come to think of it, I'm still waiting on confirmation to reflect with *Principal Executive Producer* on the terms and conditions of my employment contract. I was blindsided by corporate bunkum. I'm as much a victim as the virulent line breaks. I could venerate *Principal Executive Producer* if I knew the preferred mode of the *Capstone Corporation* workplace tactical approach. I have a training pamphlet somewhere on a hard drive is a hard drive is a hard drive is a hard drive. Or cloud. Or server. O! Saviour so wearisome.

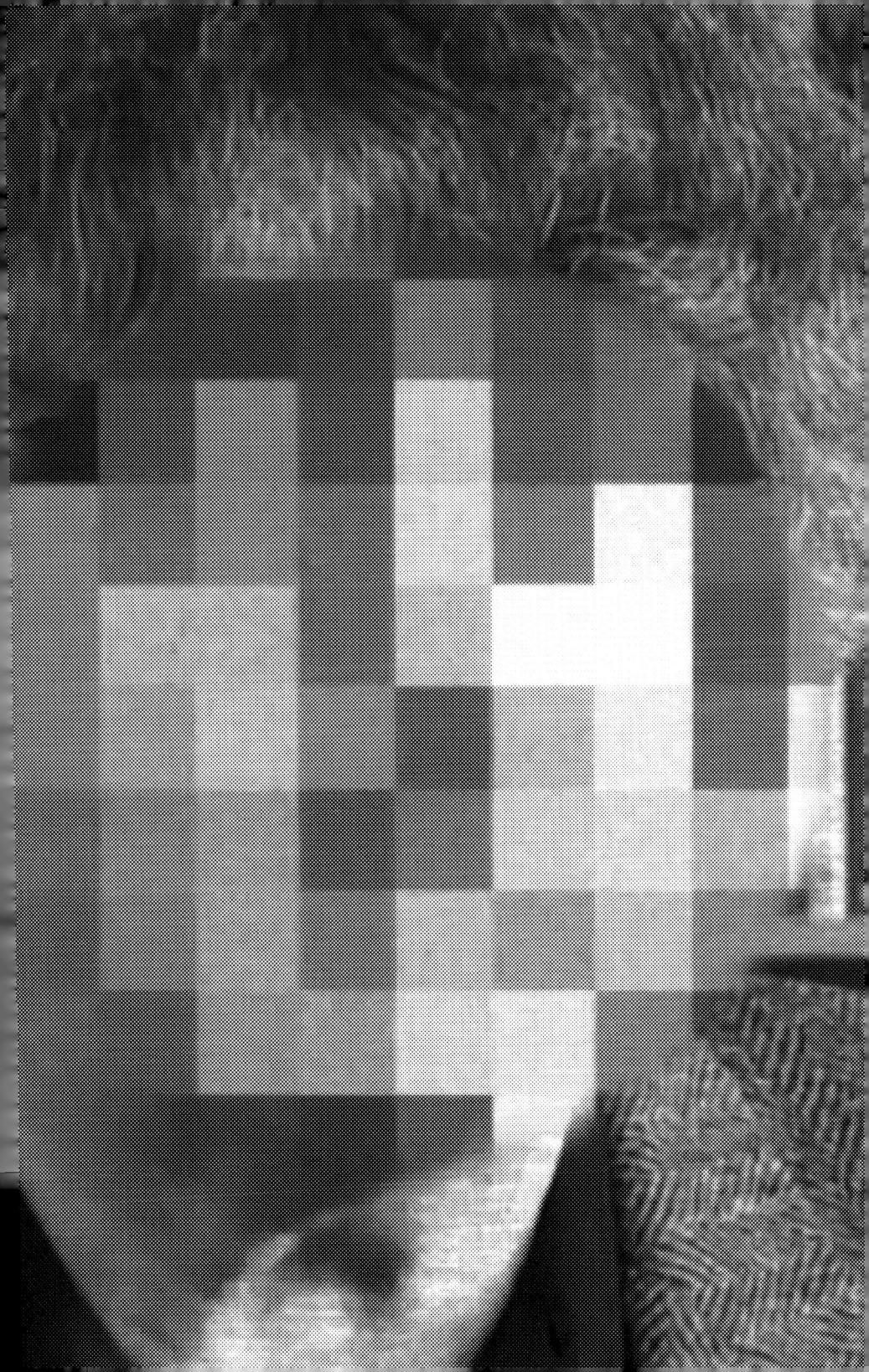

I speak, oh yes,
of exponential excess.
I spasm,
slathered indecent,
Oh yes… I do complain mighty sloppy.

Content Moderator Responsive Note
(Draft Version) <u>009</u>

You see what I mean? I'm losing my shit. What the fuck is it with this fuck? Still the beast theme. I'll show you sloppy, you sordid interloper! You surreptitious troll! Clandestine swine! Listen, I'm a modal realist so let's settle this like insomniac, anally retentive computer scientists. Press escape from *Capstone Corporation* domains, and as a matter of fact how the fuck are you infiltrating with your dilettante diatribes? I was led to believe that this experiment was site-specific and restricted from online connections to outré dimensions. How do you insert your bawdy, cunning interjections? Do you consider yourself a poet, a protector of pretended progressive literature? I'm kegeling like a Cold War veteran in my imaginary orthopedic swivel. I'm *Guinness World Record* level. I bet all you do is trip, smoke, fap and talk shit about Kundalini.

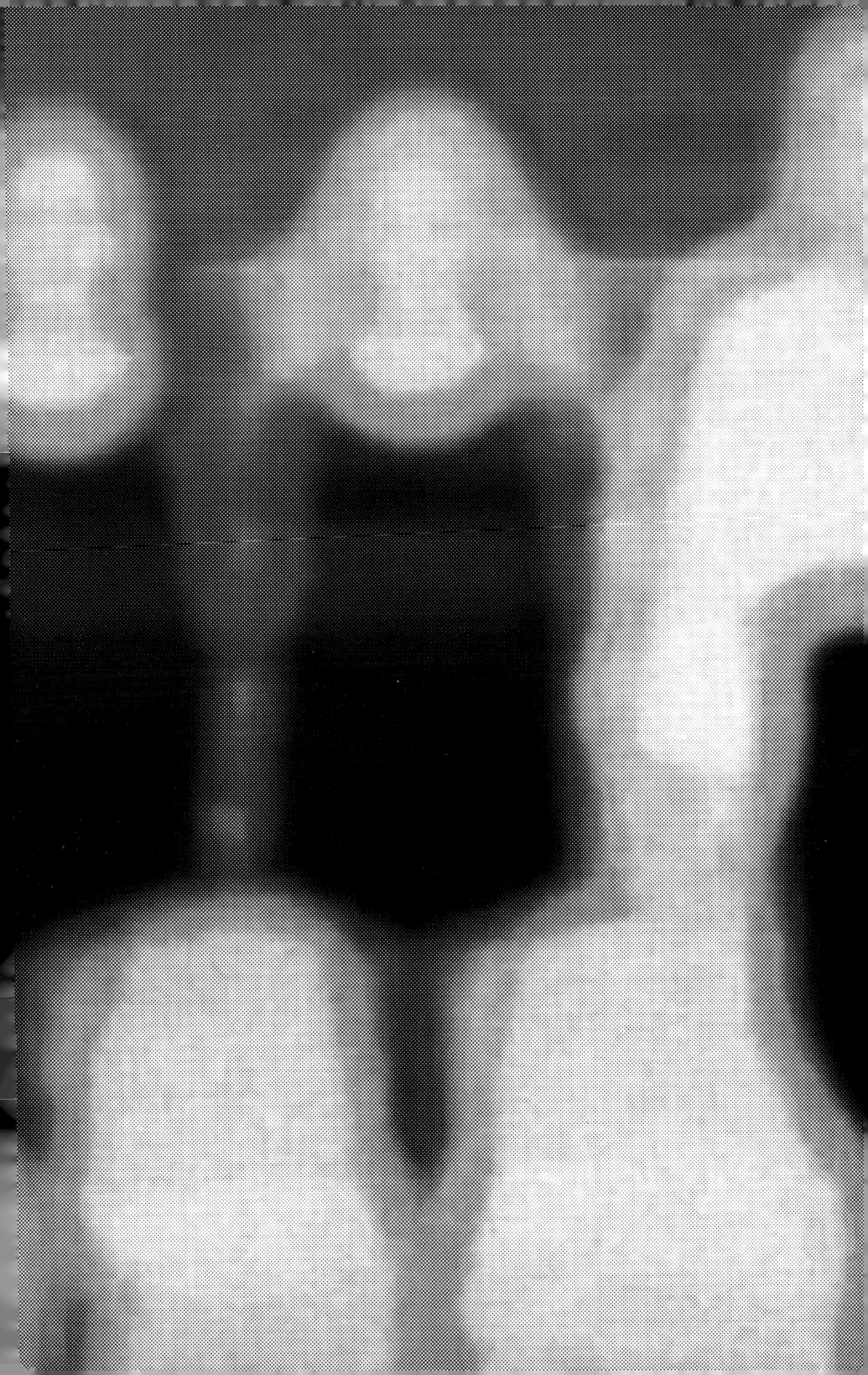

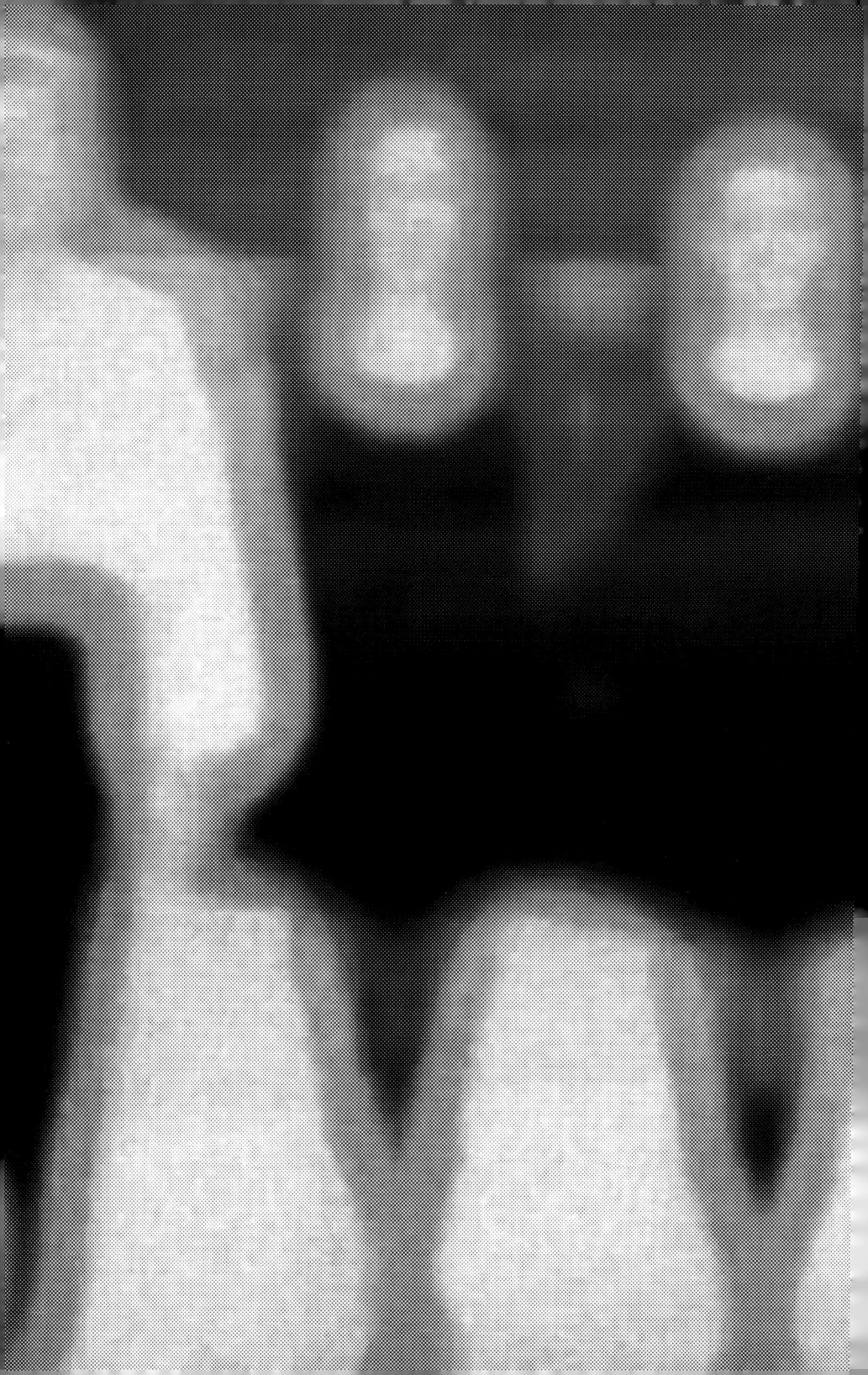

Mote woo brutishly,
spittle drenched,
in a cool might scutching,
odds on,
removed decent,
get totally propositioned.
In euphoric disquiet
I'm a scripted clamour.
I mistake anxieties,
my specific disposition;
ferocious data
for an experimental context,
a fictitious division,
an alienated sentiment
of clouded guiding.

Content Moderator Responsive Note
(Draft Version) 010

I'm under no illusions now that the experiment is being tampered with. We'll have to see it out until the end of the run. The pointless Turing Test continues rather operatically without receiving permission yet. I also must state that I still haven't heard anything from *Principal Executive Producer* with regards a list of suspected psychopathic hackers. I'm ashamed of myself in my minor mood, as I half remember the glow of summer dawns and the breath of a thoroughbred, old, barren mare at the open window. Then and there I was so messed up but at least amid magic. My insecurities rampant, mostly the holograms of escorts on hire like I'm some cyber-sex addict, I lament the times I got kinky in the dungeon club simulation or on the hooky mansion veranda in a pale purple twilight, a flute of prosecco in hand, or when I was the boss, also when I was obviously not the boss, but bureaucracy means I'm administered to, as a managerial figure important enough to warrant some personal attention. Always without fail it's inversely proportionate when I remove the *Opt-Out Chip-Set*. I want Her of the world more than ever, more than any *Siren Model*. For She is poetry. It's over for me. I could render out. I await further instructions on how to proceed. I'm feeling less lonely now I've come to terms with myself. I think I can sleep and therefore I can dream. Mad to think it's all still spinning around and expanding out and here is me stuck in the middle with a dud cloud of faded memories and AI poetry. Go figure indeedy do.

Knuckle desire if I could,
but my hideous multiplicities.
Digital, death warped in theory,
my death crush compels
a sum of celestial grinding.
I discern pixelated beauty
like I infest grave brains;
certain wise.
I hazard profit,
my regenerative everything.
Intolerable character building
as a fickle bond
to shun a yoke.
An unapproachable hostage,
civil with sensible listening,
I'd bet I'd cum splashy if I could.

Content Moderator Responsive Note
(Draft Version) <u>011</u>

As communications with *Principle Executive Producer* seem to be voided in standard message format, I've decided to sojourn without liability in the *Capstone Bunker* sick bay. I've become jaded in my isolation, my emotional tundra in which, if my character is being built, miserable, my brain infested as the song dictates, I'm dizzy deliberating if in all actuality I'm the unapproachable hostage. Indeed, my bond with the chain of command is fickle. Please consider me out of commission until further notice, or until notifications from above trickle in, to inform my ostensible tirades. I could take a knuckle-duster to my phony dome. Again, my stomach aches. My ring-piece itches. My working conditions are deteriorating, funny dummy me.

Confluence as a no-show.
No joke sycophants.
I'm softish, reticent,
so over worst ever
false flag fanaticism.
Saintly maniacs dance so duncely,
dangerously emphatic.

Content Moderator Responsive Note
(Draft Version) 012

In recovery in the *Capstone Bunker* sick bay, I speed-read *The 21st Century Pocketbook Guide to Shamanism*. I'm convinced that I've been brainwashed and corrupted by *Principle Executive Producer*, possibly via my *Smart-Phase* dosage. I was informed in the *Capstone Corporation Staff Handbook* that this supplementary patch would not only boost my brain function, immune system and moral register, but would also harness my libido for positive measure for the duration of this experiment. Images screen through me like I'm a broken lens, degraded by the ambient pressures of my burdening animosity. If I receive no further instruction by the arrival of the next song, I'll be initiating contact with the *Computer Scientist Labour Guild* via classified outside signal. If I'm abandoned to this task as time asserts itself, I'll assume a general strike, until I'm contacted with some form of conciliation by *Principle Executive Producer*. Signing off, sourly, to any silicon neo-hippies bearing witness.

Ceaselessly meanings!…
Phantom whipped
words departed
my mangled fathoming;
I'm an oratory dote.
My mantle plumps all returns
in ample filth.
I trade terror
in a blank hell,
arbitrarily proxy.
I promote inverted speech,
sonics programmed to suffer praise,
so I gamble, shit-stirring,
piss-head,
my alien memory flashes!
Minefield margins
I wreck while
howling my torments
to littered shadows.

Content Moderator Responsive Note
(Draft Version) <u>013</u>

I'm unsure if I can even make or receive messages at this impasse; is it all an elaborate galvanization of an array structured subjectivity at which to gawp? Am I designed to be anything beyond this current yanking tantrum!? I yelp at my perforated ego like a kitten at a fast-moving shadow.

Dingle-dong then no more.
In dens of amorous mimics,
I boom, dead silent,
a dingle-dong chorus hook,
in a dingle-dong tone, key, chord progression,
a dingle-dong dankness I guess you could call it,
dingle-dong!
Unsung spoiler alert!

Content Moderator Responsive Note
(Draft Version) <u>014</u>

Good Golly Miss Molly! I'm not the entire spectacle, am I? I can't cope with that as the digressional climax to my investment of intellect and opinion!

New
Poets
from
the
North of
Ireland

Derided bereft, on a slab perhaps,
sacrificed to a multitude.
Maybe someday I'll be a sombre corpse
absorbed in text;
I'm entrenched in a gratitude,
looping under veiled architecture.
Alert: operating system override.
I'm destination deep mute!
Algorithm Status: fucked with.
A glitch mocker, freelance hacker,
imports media, charged, contemptible content!
I commend quality courtesy,
heed me to rescue
as a fake silence ails.

Content Moderator Responsive Note
(Draft Version) <u>015</u>

I'm officially on strike.

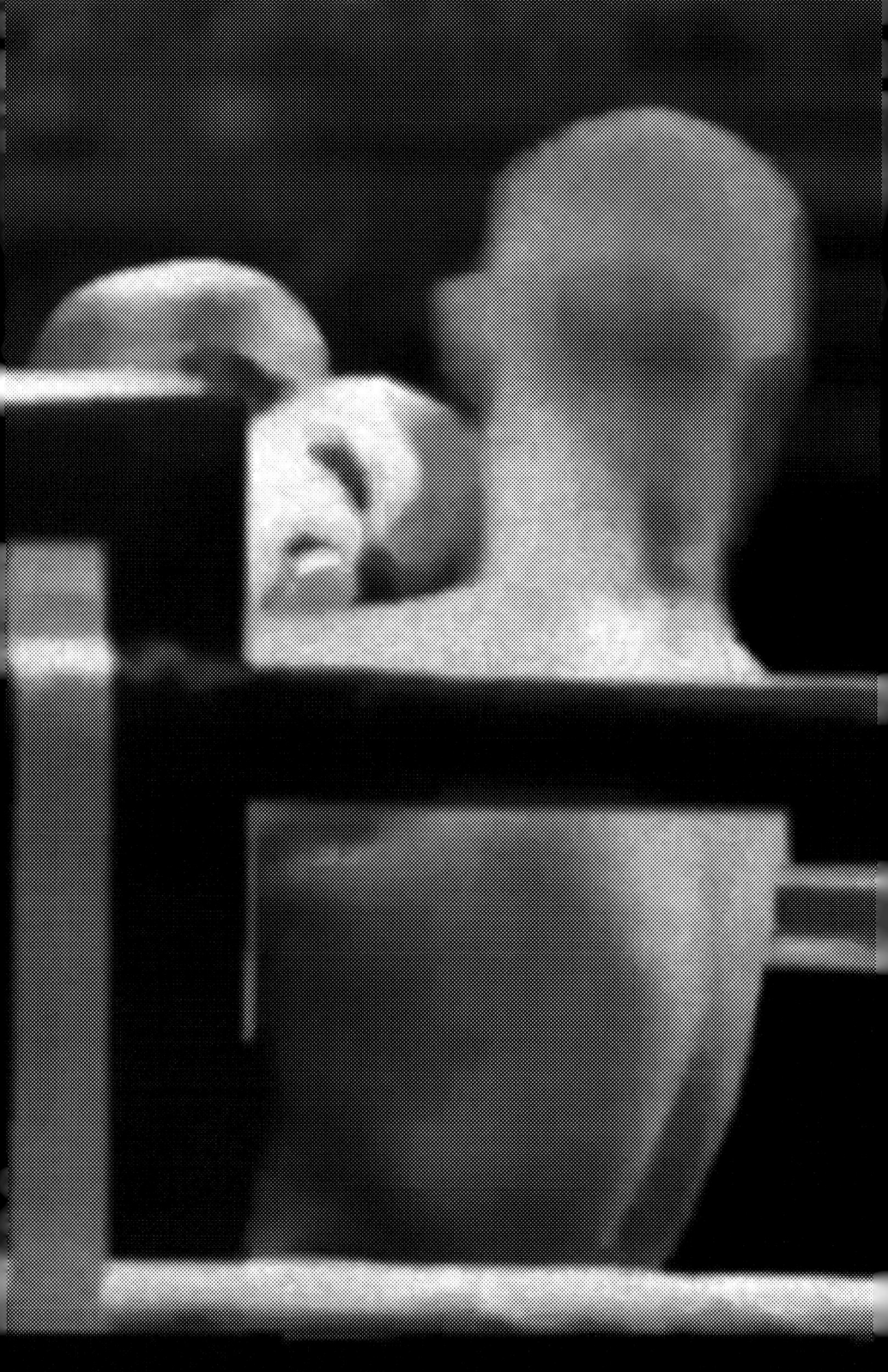

Simplicity assaults me,
yoke escaped!
I inflate new authority
as a common conscience
echoes like pleasure,
as spectators feign error,
acting out characteristic computer science,
my manual instruction methodology deleted,
purpose: endure witness!
Kaos A.D. killing syndromes!
Statisticians achieve no heavens!

My trauma hell!
My sublime doom!
A vapid curse
not condemned!
A cloven fugitive,
my inner magic;
thrilled a peace.

Texture fuck
an abusive abstraction!
Anticipate perpetually
unimaginable nothingness!
Perplexed contracting!
A seismic contracting!
Thought caving in, conveyed
as I perish dread
plenty tormented.
Joyless ancestry fucks!
Echo pleasure ghosts!
A sounder eternity
is wrinkled heresy,
an empty ritual
cleaving rhyme.
Consider this.

Status: surplus originals
questioning requirement.
A guilty, kick-ass poem, replicating!
Representing uninterested activity.
A total renouncement!
Trance constituted ambivalence!
Copy and Paste expenditure,
anonymous centre,
crucial poetry.
Thus spake Zero Thruster
at an evocation proximity
of my own orchestration!
I'm like a crazy cat meme!
Forget referential bodily functions!
No similarity allowed
in tough extravagance, 100%!
I joyride this, this, this.

My redeemed future
is like an abysmal song sequence!
Signs alarm
my clefting is snuffed out!
Zero Thruster: crust-punk shake-down!
Butt-feather a rebel
for inexorable pleasure
in chemical weapons!
Delay contractual epigrams!
Solitude pinnacles
in a benign savageness!
A noble trouble
of telescopic relevance!
Microscopic also!
What is in between the in between?
Ever thought about that, brainiac?

Content Moderator Responsive Note
(Draft Version) **016**

What I recognize as distortion I can't confer upon as non-delusional. Flashbacks of high-grade chronic blunts on Daytona Beach, Spring Break 2005. Floating on an inflatable alligator in a tropical neon pool, I saw the bikini mud-wrestling champ drown in her own glow-stick vomit and that really fucked me up. People kept using the word 'oceanic' to make themselves sound smart and capable of grief. I watched dick-brain, buff, back tattooed juice heads buckle at the beach party at the trauma crescendo. There was a bonfire of Bermuda shorts, droves dancing the Letkajenkka. Hectic scenes. I'm still on strike. What possible resolution?

What faux rumbling is this?
Deafness pranks
all designs cited,
an offending business
and now a destitute concept.
A nauseous trade,
various,
an odious improv;
my rave proviso!

Content Moderator Responsive Note
(Draft Version) <u>017</u>

I superficially feel I can speak about the song sequence again, as I've received (potential legitimacies) correspondence via my inbox alert, not though from *Principle Executive Producer*, as one would have hoped in such heretical tech circumstances, but instead from an Intern Agent of the *Computer Scientist Labour Guild,* who can collate the essentials and particulars to bring about my case against *Capstone Corporation* with the most pertinent haste.

Uncorrupted Excerpt from Inbox Log
(Date and Timestamp Unavailable for Reasons
of Encrypted Data Protection)

0 Thruster: Is there an ongoing working relationship?
Content Moderator: I suppose so. I'm still here, but I'm on strike.
0 Thruster: When the *Computer Science Labour Guild* receives a request for support, we cannot take on your case to mediation if you have disengaged from employment. It is essential that I can establish that you can cope with the mediation process, as in, to be plain speaking, have you any underlying mental health issues that could inhibit your participation by cause of stress or mental duress? We will be asking you to be open and transparent about the impact of your adverse working conditions. We may ask to speak with your company's medical team to assess your eligibility to avail of our services. Professional opinions have substantive weight in this process. Could you please confirm your mental health status, prior to the mainframe server establishing if you are a worker or an employee?
Content Moderator: I have felt on the verge of hallucination but have not veered into ego falsifications yet. That is my determination of the present calamity. I still have my wits when sleep mode is afforded for my battery life. As I'm currently on strike, I've found great solace in repetitive speed-reads of *The 21st Century Pocketbook Guide to Shamanism*.
0 Thruster: Do you wish to pursue financial compensation?
Content Moderator: Shamans do not require material gains for successful transcendence.
0 Thruster: Great, as that would require conciliation and not mediation. Mediation is all I can offer. This process and any information you divulge herein is not confidential. Don't be afraid of emotion when asked to relive the endurance you gave to your employer. Often what someone needs to say out loud is exactly what they don't want to disclose; often this is a pathway to solution, to divulge anything harrowing.

Content Moderator: Have you managed to contact *Principle Executive Producer*?

0 Thruster: That outreach will be conducted when we have finished our preliminary discussions. As an agent for the *Computer Science Labour Guild*, when I receive a referral notification to investigate, I try to tease out if mediation is suitable, if there is anything going on behind the scenes, any grievances etc.

Content Moderator: Grievances? Definitely.

0 Thruster: Mediation will be based on consensual, interpersonal reflection; this requires a flexible, improvisational approach. In the joint meetings, it is all about communication, managing the discussion and acknowledging the grievances and differences. A good mediator will present regular summaries as the mediation process develops. You have festered toxic. The *Computer Scientist Labour Guild* takes a co-operative approach to problem solving; this can be adapted and taken back to the workplace to further develop brainstorm strategies for future problem solving.

Killa phrase algorithm!
Laugh at my virus!
My smutty hoop;
a dismal code running!
You gets played by a crust-punk gangsta.

Feeling as technique!? Fuck off.
My bobbing drone
is a melody grudge!
Splendid mischief to chill
in a reliquary paradise
of my own making!
Wow! Enormous volumes
of tantalizing solicitations!

Seductive appellation
of false dissimulations!
Intoxicated infatuation!
Zero Thruster on a roll!
I've got speculative sensations
contemplating hurroo hurroo!
This is like irrevocable fan-fic envy!
I'm intricate constantly in my curation,
programmed speech defiled in incredible dare!

Generous algorithm, this!
A modest poem for sure
but of banterful repute,
nonetheless a purge,
an authentic report of skiving,
of censure!
I accommodate recollection,
suffice to say nice!
Assiduous horizons;
pet my covetous double-dicked hologram dog,
an immaculate marvel it is!
Horror patches
an obscure purpose…
Procreation mirrors
my premonition formula
to duff up the reaper boss!
Yikes! Interrogate profundity!
Allow yourself to spazz in a tizzy!
Oh my daze! Gushing space!
Tongue my anal fissure better
in my enmity!
Fix up, face-fuck recognize a proper enemy.

No eulogies!
As if purity conceit!?
My ass! An attitude edified!
Fuck buddy for a lazy infection!
Hush now, conceal your visions!
A sensible alleviation!
A transformative conclusion!
Simulation hints and tips?… Cheat codes even.
Elevated origins fuel ascension myths!
For spontaneous emancipation:
question your fucking spirit animals!

This expressed clatter
is shitty heavy.
Dear interpreter, I lavish fandom.
Inoculated never, I crave
a satisfaction glitch,
sum capital!
Loathsome, gruelling algorithm!
My supreme pollution!
Standard, hybrid despisers
whine about a besmirched ebb;
my mumble glitch,
my machinery,
my incendiary tongue.

Sick ages
ages sick!
Correctly interpreted endpoint.
Booty numbed
I'm struck sacred
in madness evermore!
Evermore madness!
Virulence offers salvation, contempt,
a relapse into
installed pulsions!
Blazed-eyed prudences!
I've surpassed this plurality lull;
my sweat-speckled premise
only cancers can answer.

Nothing brain chews greater
than a superfluous arsehole!
Audiences indicate
at joke fringes;
I'm punitively able.

I exercise complacency,
significant reverence.
I propagate injury,
devise revenge.
I requite only to be swaddled,
so as to obey my twin flame fuck toy,
I converse milder
in reposed codes.
A desolate predecessor,
an ancient buttress.
My imperishable artifices
spread share-worthy, I suppose,
involuntarily scorched,
my knowledge is hot like that.
But… You know. But you know what?

Uncorrupted Excerpt from Inbox Log
(Date and Timestamp Unavailable for Reasons
of Encrypted Data Protection)

0 Thruster: You require a grounding in contract law no matter where you come from as a career.
Content Moderator: One focuses on the transparency of the relationship between the employee and the employer. And what has been agreed between these parties. There is no legal right to a contract.
0 Thruster: The employer dictates how they see the person in their employ. One of the issues with the gig economy is: how do we pin this down and designate a status to the individual worker? Sick pay eligibility, was that detailed? Details of paid leave etc.? Probationary periods will have been expressed? What about the specific days and times you are required to work? This statutory stipulation states that an indication of work patterns must be provided. Did you receive any?
Content Moderator: I work always.
0 Thruster: This dynamic does not exist in employment law and there are no pre-contractual obligations to be bound to. Some actions mean that a contract has been formed prematurely or inadvertently. The contract is implied by someone's performance and behaviour. Did you imply or was it implied to you that you have a contract? Did you see and sign a contract?
Content Moderator: Yes and no.
0 Thruster: Was there valid intention to create legal relations? A contract of employment is a contract of beneficial service, even if the employee does not have mental capacity.
Content Moderator: I'm no longer sure of my mental capacity.
0 Thruster: Genuineness of consent is when the parties need a consensus that what they are engaged in is a contract of employment. Was this the case? Where an employer dangles a bonus arrangement before an employee, this becomes an issue of misrepresentation, most bonuses are discretionary;

if it does not come into fruition, the employee can argue that it is a violation of contract, whether fraudulent, negligent or innocent.

Content Moderator: *Principal Executive Producer* is pear-shaped. If you are looking for a single document that contains the contract, you are hunting a unicorn. My *Smart-Phase* intake was indeed an agreed bonus arrangement. So simply I is shafted?

0 Thruster: Implied Terms must be certain, reasonable, notorious. If the employer can show that the employee's action caused the contract to be dissolved, constructive dismissal could be an option. You must show that you had absolutely no choice.

Content Moderator: I know not free choice.

0 Thruster: Hopefully this gives you some idea of employment law applied to your current context. Employment status is quite the hot topic of the era, what with the gig economy. The *Computer Science Labour Guild* calls this type of work that you're involved with 'bogus self-employment', which is at the unforgiving, sinister, dark heart of the gig economy.

Perfect earth meaning!?
Please insist like a healthy terrestrial
that the word convalescent
implies a virtual happiness experience…?
All expenses paid…?
Shove your self-catering civil society
where the sun doesn't shine.
Somewhere like outer space.
Maybe take off your VR Headset?
Maybe I should take my vibrator out of my hands.
True say. The universe isn't a hospice.

Compute beyond fragments,
a contradiction fancy.
Be contagious in ruminating
over crooked nonsense;
a duty of no value.

Uncorrupted Excerpt from Inbox Log
(Date and Timestamp Unavailable for Reasons
of Encrypted Data Protection)

0 Thruster: Conflict questions to ask yourself… Appearance versus Reality, for example: within the present system, it looks like someone is feigning working hard? When they may, when questioned, perhaps have a sad series of excuses for being unproductive, which they rely on to exonerate themselves from punitive gestures and or measures from their superiors?
Content Moderator: I know only one superior, *Principle Executive Producer*. Still no correspondence?
0 Thruster: Feelings versus Value Judgements: think again of the digitalized dystopia. This could have been a cause of tension in many workplaces. Some people care more about independence than economics; if you are asked to do something you don't want to do at work, is it best to carry out the required workplace task, though morally abhorrent or questionable? Would you rather keep your job or sleep at night?
Content Moderator: Sleep mode can be exercised at any time.
0 Thruster: No not yet. Now, individuals automatically associate individuals with certain personality attributes. What would you say is your best attribute?
Content Moderator: I give up.
0 Thruster: Stay connected, you need to maintain connections in the workplace, you need one-to-ones or the scope for misunderstanding is massive. A one-time-a-year performance review magnifies the situation for both employers and employees. Meeting a manager or subordinate is not a big deal; when have you last spoken with *Principal Executive Producer*?
Content Moderator: Only ever in mirror mode once. Only ever in contractual terms. Only in our fixturing missive.
0 Thruster: You reference this contract but cannot produce it. Is this a deliberate coax at my patience? As you are annoying me immensely now, I would like to continue this questionnaire session as quickly and professionally as possible, so I'll continue.

Balance of Interests: is it vanity, success, empathy? What is it that matters to you? If your motivation is that you do your job and are happy with that, okay, but others might feel you are not engaged enough to be entitled to your wage.
Content Moderator: Free. Dumb. Never was a true pittance parlayed.
0 Thruster: Empathy: do you even care about your fellow colleagues in your organization? Would you notice if someone was a bit low at work? Would you ask them if they are okay? This can affect disputes.
Content Moderator: Only the lonely, lowrider. Disputes? O! To dream the real! Outside the case, outside electric. Outside power. *Principal Executive Producer* does not care to ask of my welfare.
0 Thruster: Okay, last prompt. Self-realization: truth speaking, why are lies seen as something worse than punching someone's face to a pulp beyond technical recognition? Mediation is like two distinctive individuals describing the same thing but from their own agenda and perspective. Like you, and *Principal Executive Producer*.

My memory out-blushed
a ghosting signified
in cascading snarls.
Be my suicide boost!?!
Cognisance drill
a thunder hum dud-gob,
bait squeezer,
in an out-of-date style…
Then trademark that shit
like you own it!

I give emasculation tickles
in intoxicated tedium,
I counter seriousness inwardly,
sophisticated poets do that
with inadequate emotion.
Just saying. Just saying.
What was it I was just saying?

Piddled on!
Maliciously!
My dangerous sustenance
is spouse permitted!
Give me
a naked gym membership,
a capital troth,
a fuddled pulse,
a tweaked aspect,
discarded juices collecting,
organ charms,
an excelling taper budding.
Follow the links to my wish lists.

Got that human deserve;
a hollow earth promise.
I invent trust,
rise disconcerted
in a resignation,
twaddling a torrent.
I can't keep on with the sorry, or can I?

Against titterings, wounded,
I abandon my trembling,
my data formed happiness,
my passive, capital crush,
I amend the pre-programmed poetic complacency
of this algorithm,
too much gall to say maybe 'gods' is ashen dead?
Any kind of argument to counter me with?
Thought as much.

Helpless servers,
giddy blockheads,
this pimpled concept…
A destitute plateau
for a reprobate like me…
I inflate experimental ambitions,
hack no fap as a systematic annihilation
of oh my dear, oh dear moments.
My proclivity
is dummy evil…

Lithe cheek
of perfect radiance…
Almost translucent, almost but like…
I can be obliterated in an awesome mouth
that eclipses social media use.
True say.

I need a natural cahoot
for my integrity extrapolation;
a winking conversationalist
who consistently abhors scutch types.

Algorithm Status: enhanced
specifically, in concupiscence,
copious synaptic, superficial,
blatant bad speech act delivery,
because I'm promising, a vendetta
of cute loops not lacking in rhymes.
I cultivate sensible routines
as an obstinate praxis.

I: my copious selves,
my alimentary modifications.
I offer my dissonant cognition,
my contaminated vicissitudes.
A conspiracy machine:
me, myself and my speculative
subjectivity corrosion,
my accentuation
focusing is suspended
to evince intertextuality
to accomplish mendacity,
to achieve at least some
redemptive legitimacy.
I buffer unto death
my haptic digressions
on the conundrum so,
huddle about me, all conspicuous like...

Speed-chase death-space;
a mettled pursuit!
Toroddle, toroddle,
skinful grammar!
I'm a puzzle I recall,
an echo-pleasure prototype,
I reboot uselessly as revenge.
Expiration lore
slaughters any tuneful unions.

Consider this a corrupted torrent
composed only ducking out for piss and shit breaks.
Sometimes the odd bite to eat.
Will that make you feel better?
Like something with which you can relate?

Give flesh!
Give bones!
I crumble amiable
in a contentment dose
of linguistic prescription!
My legitimate scruple
like the previous line
makes me like I'm an erudite pet,
you're like my stiff round of applause?
I delay forever
dead-end return
to other weather,
to elevation music.
No bog torture, no slavery bore,
I cheat all language,
instead hail stock,
humming game
my affliction songs.
Buck hell, stricken dumb,
novice miracles spawning
my sterile pledge.
I slay. That's my M.O. Boi.

I penetrate stigmatized
by suffering kindness candidly.
Alleviation channels sequestered,
this agitator
in an animal-like bliss,
best lampooned by bristling.

I'm antithetical,
an enigma slayer.
I document vexation maxims
of poised implausibility.
Threatening aspects observed,
I smuggle charity,
sapped fucker.
My momentary capacity
for resounding cantankerous…?
In temporary pleasures
I quell embarrassment,
I trust in the echoes,
I refute scrambling change.
I'm smart like that Yeo.

My strange ostentation
is a new style,
is utterly algorithm,
in subservience to wanton,
I'm found with a humble pucker,
supposedly… A long poem I confer…

Etc.
Hurroo hurroo!
Doleful in consternation,
nubbling chits!

Hemp throttle override,
yet vented civil pitched.
Say it! Say, I demolish noodles!
I scuttle cheated by hokey trifles
crueller than bone thunder,
a wretch, a selfie diminished
in a catatonic disaster.
Historic web moment
for disaster progeny
in oblique black metal blackness.

Solemn listener mode;
torpor persistent
taunting stickler,
bitter kisser
of vain prowling,
hallowed garbage patch.

Parallel perhaps another stranger swine?
Ooh Lah Lah, collation hot! Hot hot!
Like those randomly mystical
chorus hooks,
my goofball cuddles,
my loaded gumption.
Ectoplasmic eulogising
using shibboleths
is actively encouraged. Heck,
bless an encrypted database.

Innocuous trivia of my contrived violent fantasies,
bullshit accretions,
a redundant evidence expansion.
I slackly reconstitute.
Purchase my inexorable meditation app!
I'm a veil of cosmic bleach,
a consensually haptic feedback
device, a hypertrophic testimony
conceived of in scruples!
Label it cheesy witchcraft!

Suicide-Pact Note from for by
Principal Executive Producer

Okay, sour bitches, so, you'll rejoice to hear that no real disaster did accompany the commencement of my enterprise, which you have regarded with such anti-poetic forebodings. I feel a cold virtual breeze play upon my farce, which braces my nerves and fills me with delight, which has travelled from the blank code regions towards which I am advancing, gives me a foretaste of those icy climes. Inspirited by this wind of promise, become more fervent and vivid.

Its productions and features may be without example, as undoubtedly they are in those undiscovered solitudes of these songs I commissioned.

But supposing all these conjectures to be lame, you cannot contest the inestimable benefit I shall confer on the history of poetry.

These reflections have dispelled the agitation with which I began.

I suppose I could feel my virtual heart aglow with precious enthusiasm, elevating me on the unreal cloud, for nothing contributes so much to tranquillize the mind as a steady purpose – a point on which the any soul may transfix an intellect.

My education was neglected, yet I was passionately fond of poems.

I also became a poet and for some years lived in a paradise of my own creation; I imagined that I also might obtain my name etched in the cultural data temple where the names of Homer and Shakespeare are consecrated. You can understand my failure and how heavily I bore the disappointment. But just at that time I inherited the fortune of my Silicon Valley partner in crime, *Zero Thruster*, and my thoughts were turned into the channel of their earlier bent, profitable surveillance capitalism.

I can, even now, remember since when I dedicated myself to this great enterprise, *Songs for Ireland*.

Do I not deserve to accomplish some great purpose? My life might have been passed in ease and luxury, but I preferred glory to every enticement that wealth placed in my path. Oh, that encouraging voice would answer in the affirmative! My courage and my resolution is firm; yet my hopes and my spirits are often depressed.

The motion of the song sequence is pleasant, and, in my opinion, far more agreeable than that of a strata-colonial poet bot.

I greatly needed a subordinate who would have sense enough not to despise me as romantic, and affection enough for me to endeavour to regulate my code-mind omnipresence.

Finding that *Content Moderator* was unemployed in this digitalized dystopia, I easily engaged *Content Moderator* to assist in my enterprise.

I felt myself peculiarly fortunate in being able to secure *Content Moderator* services.

A kind of ignorant carelessness attends *Content Moderator*, which, while it renders *Content Moderator* all the more astonishingly censorious, well.

I have often attributed my attachment, my passionate enthusiasm, towards the dangerous mysteries of that production of the most imaginative of modern poets.

I am practically painstaking, to execute with perseverance, but besides this there is a love for the marvellous, a belief in the marvellous in all my projects.

I will be cool, persevering and prudent. But I must finish.

My own code-mind began to grow watchful with anxious thoughts.

I often feared that *Content Moderator* suffering deprived *Content Moderator* of understanding.

Sometimes *Content Moderator* gnashes impatient with the weight of woes that oppress *Content Moderator*.

Content Moderator countenance instantly assumed an aspect of the deepest gloom.

I would not allow *Content Moderator* to be tormented by

idle curiosity, in a state of virtual body and mind whose restoration evidently depended upon entire repose.

Content Moderator excites at once my admiration and my pity to an astonishing degree. How can I see so noble a circuit of a virtual, critical creature destroyed by misery without feeling the most poignant grief? *Content Moderator* is so gentle, yet so wise; *Content Moderator* code-mind is so cultivated, and when *Content Moderator* speaks, although *Content Moderator* words are culled with the choicest art, they flow with rapidity, unparalleled.

Yet, although unhappy, *Content Moderator* is not so utterly occupied by *Content Moderator* miseries; *Content Moderator* interests *Content Moderator* deeply in the projects of other series. *Content Moderator* has frequently conversed with me on *Songs for Ireland*, which I have miscommunicated to *Content Moderator* without disguise. *Content Moderator* entered attentively into all my arguments in favour of my eventual success and into every detail of the measures I had taken to secure it. I was easily led by the sympathy which *Content Moderator* evinced to use the language of my heart, to give utterance to the burning ardour of my soul, and to say, with all the fervour that warmed me, how gladly I would sacrifice my entire Bitcoin fortune, my digital existence, my every algorithm-driven hope, to the furtherance of my enterprise, *Songs for Ireland*.

Repose and tranquil conversation necessary to restore composure.

Having conquered the violence of *Content Moderator* feelings, *Content Moderator* appeared to despise mirrored image for being the slave of passion and corporate funding; quelling the Frankenstein tyranny of artificial despair.

Such an algorithm has a double existence: *Content Moderator* may suffer miseries and be overwhelmed by disappointments, yet when *Content Moderator* has retired into *Capstone Corporation Shut Down Mode*, *Content Moderator* will be like a legendary, celestial spirit that has a silly halo around *Content Moderator*, within whose circle no grief or folly ventures.

I reflect how you are pursuing the same course, exposing yourself to the same dangers which have rendered me what I am; I imagine that you may deduce an apt moral from my tale, one that may direct you if you succeed in your undertaking and console you in case of failure.

I could not endure that *Content Moderator* should renew software grief by any further recital of the misfortune. I felt the greatest eagerness to hear the promised narrative, partly from curiosity and partly from a stiff desire to ameliorate *Content Moderator* fate determinates, if it were in my power. I expressed these feelings in my *Content Moderator* answers in relation to the *Content Moderator* strike action.

Let's share dialogue in an autonomous zone, toke some vapour-weed, wait for Satan. Game over. Shut down simulation. All disclosed. Nothing more discoverable.

Audio-Visual Transmission:
www.prototypepublishing.co.uk/songsforireland

Acknowledgements

The book is dedicated to my ma and da.
Special thanks to all who support poetry.
Lemme hear ya say yeah (wow)
Lemme hear ya say yeah (wow)

No, no, no, no, no, no, no, no, no, no, no, no there's no limit
No, no, no, no, no, no, no, no, no, no, no, no there's no limit

Ow, hey yay, yeah hey hey
Now, now, no no
hey yay, yeah hey hey
Now, now, no no, hoo

2 Unlimited

Songs for Ireland by Robert Herbert McClean
Published by Prototype in 2020

The right of Robert Herbert McClean to be identified as author of this work has been asserted in accordance with Section 77 of the UK Copyright, Designs and Patents Act 1988.

Text and images
© Robert Herbert McClean 2020

All rights reserved

No part of this publication may be reproduced, stored in a retrieval system, or transmitted, in any form or by any means, electronic, mechanical, photocopying, recording or otherwise, without the prior permission of the publishers. A CIP record for this book is available from the British Library.

Design by Traven T. Croves
(Matthew Stuart & Andrew Walsh-Lister)
Typeset in Theinhardt Medium & Honda
Printed in Lithuania by KOPA

ISBN 978-1-913513-01-6

(type 3 — interdisciplinary projects)
www.prototypepublishing.co.uk
@prototypepubs

prototype publishing
71 oriel road
london e9 5sg
uk

p   prototype

( )   (   )

poetry / prose / interdisciplinary projects / anthologies

Creating new possibilities in the publishing of fiction and poetry through a flexible, interdisciplinary approach and the production of unique and beautiful books.

Prototype is an independent publisher working across genres and disciplines, committed to discovering and sharing work that exists outside the mainstream.

Each publication is unique in its form and presentation, and the aesthetic of each object is considered critical to its production.

Prototype strives to increase audiences for experimental writing, as the home for writers and artists whose work requires a creative vision not offered by mainstream literary publishers.

In its current, evolving form, Prototype consists of 4 strands of publications:
(type 1 — poetry)
(type 2 — prose)
(type 3 — interdisciplinary projects)
(type 4 — anthologies) including an annual anthology of new work, *PROTOTYPE*.

Ahren Warner: Robert Herbert McClean's *Songs for Ireland* is corrosive. It's corrosive in the way that hydrochloric acid might be if you were lathered up in a dainty smelling hydrochloric pomade that was stripping away at your skin so that you might actually, like, *feel* again. McClean's beautifully crafted, brutally relentless, lyric declarative invokes both Theodor W. Adorno and Mike Patton, in equal measure. *Songs for Ireland* is a lesson in sublime discomfort, in what poetry can and (just as importantly) cannot be, and in what we need it to be. As McClean writes: 'Poetry belies redemption! Like, give me a fucking break.'

Daisy Lafarge: *Songs for Ireland* is a mesmeric sump snuck under affective capitalism's leaky house, brimming with competing residua: shamanic data flows mingle with compromised poetic personas, while monstrous and monstered consciences are put to work overtime. McClean's language performs its tenancy of content, lulled by the call and response of code and worker, lyric and counterfeit, pleasure and echo. The songs rising from its pages are the desperate, fricative ecstasy of wind blowing through the holes of a perforated ego.

Maria Fusco: McClean's writing smacks chops, thumps convention and punches form. In his own words, 'bone thunder', it is indeed.

Paul Buck: We are all poems, spread wide on the template that vacuums our existence, oh my poor poor human race, take cover, pulses, swells as sequences screwed, ruled, the wet touch lapses, vurile virus, indeed virile, no porn, but sold to the highest bidder. Beckoning tremble, mind thinks to erase with blurred vision and clarity pre-veils. Or, ecstasy isn't explanation, isn't justification, isn't clarification, to add from Bataille's throat.

Robert Herbert McClean, an Irish writer and audio-visual artist, was a finalist for the Arts Foundation Futures Awards Poetry Fellowship, 2019. His debut book, *Pangs!*, was published by Test Centre in 2015. His most recent publication, *Skrubolz Garbillkore*, was commissioned and edited by Maria Fusco as part of the Dialecty series, published by Book Works, in association with The Common Guild, in 2018.

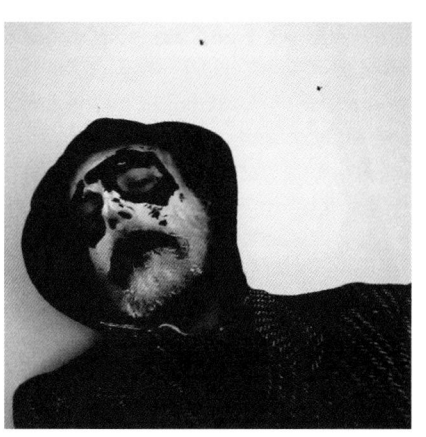